Shadows Standing Over Me

Tribulations

BOOK 2

LADY J.

authorHOUSE

AuthorHouse™
1663 Liberty Drive
Bloomington, IN 47403
www.authorhouse.com
Phone: 833-262-8899

Published by AuthorHouse 09/29/2021

ISBN: 978-1-6655-3844-2 (sc)
ISBN: 978-1-6655-3843-5 (e)

Print information available on the last page.

Any people depicted in stock imagery provided by Getty Images are models, and such images are being used for illustrative purposes only. Certain stock imagery © Getty Images.

This book is printed on acid-free paper.

CONTENTS

Chapter 1 Taking Care of Home..1

Chapter 2 In My Mother's House..3

Chapter 3 A Boy Named King...5

Chapter 4 Just Like Your Father..7

Chapter 5 Going To School..11

Chapter 6 Anxiety from school...14

Chapter 7 Kicked Out..17

Chapter 8 Last Chance...19

Chapter 9 Miss BlackHamilton..22

Chapter 10 Our One And Only..25

Chapter 11 Looking For Daddy..27

Chapter 12 The Picture On The Wall...30

Chapter 13 Good And Bad News..32

Chapter 14 He Is The Father..33

Chapter 15 The Fall...35

Chapter 16 1981..37

Chapter 17 A New House..40

Chapter 18 Time on my hands..42

Chapter 19 Moving...44

Chapter 20 Making My Bed Hard..47

Chapter 21 No Money More problems...53

Chapter 22 My casa is your casa...56

Chapter 23 Love and War..58

Chapter 24 I Mean No Disrespect...62

Chapter 25 Where Do I Go From Here..66

Chapter 26 June 25, 1985..69

Chapter 27 Somebody Got To Go..70

Chapter 28 Dr. Jekyll And Mr. Hyde..73

Chapter 29 Up In Smoke...79

Chapter 30 The Beginning Of The End..82

CHAPTER 1

Taking Care of Home

She began to let go.

I finally talked her down off of the bridge and we walked home.

My Mother had to go to the hospital because of a gunshot wound.

After this, I began to pay more and more attention to her. I felt like I had to take care of her.

Emotionally and Mentally she wasn't strong enough at this point.

There would be days when I would go to school and still worry about her.

Thinking about what she was doing and if she was okay.

I had to help look after my sisters and take care of them until she felt better.

I watched her pick herself up from a lonely painful place.

At that time I felt my mother's pain, cried with and for her.

When things would hurt me, I would think if my Father was here this wouldn't happen.

To this day I feel that way until someone proves me wrong.

Mother was sleeping all day and she would be up all night.

I would go into her room after she fell asleep just to check on her and make sure she was breathing.

Removing the burned-out cigarette still in her hand while blowing out the candles that she left burning.

She would be sleeping peacefully with a broken heart.

I remember telling myself that I was never going to be with a man like that.

A man that would hurt me and just walk away.

Over the next few years, my relationship with my mother began to change as I got older.
Most of the time I felt like she didn't love me as much as she did my sisters.

I was the Oldest and most of the responsibility was put on me.
Cleaning, cooking, and looking after my sisters.
I was babysitting so much that I started babysitting for my mother's friends when they wanted to go out.

From one end of the Bottom to the other. The Westside too!

Babysitting also puts me in situations where I had to protect the kids I was taking care of.
To witness a man physically put his hands on a woman in front of her children, let alone in front of me I'll never forget that day.

The fear from that day has kept me connected to those children for life.

Living in the Projects it was always something happening that would make me think, or should I say ask the question "Why".
That very thing, asking why, would also be the reason that my Mother and I would clash.

CHAPTER 2

In My Mother's House

I can only speak on this because' Today I understand.

As I got older I began to have a voice and I would discuss family matters with Grandmother, something I always did.

The relationship that I had with my Grandmother was a relationship I hope to have with my grandchildren.

My Grandmother was my "ROCK" my "Everything".

Her smile is something that I miss however I can see.

I would talk with her about any and everything including my Mother.

From a young child, my Grandparent' house was always a safe place for me.

And that's where I would run to when something happened.

When my mother would punish me.

At times it was so bad that I would run from her.

I was afraid of what she would do to me. She would pick up anything and hit me with it.

I know what it feels like to get hit in the head and see stars. Knots on my arms from trying to block her from hitting me with whatever she had in her hand.

I wish I knew who and where my father was.

I would run away.

A few times I ran away to the Gaither's Funeral Home.

Mrs.Giather was my friend and she owned The funeral home.

Whenever in passing, if by chance she was where I could see her she would let me come in and talk to her.

In the evening Mrs.Gaither would stand in front of the picture window at the funeral home and watch the kids run up and down the street.

The Other children were afraid, they knew that's where they took the dead people.

Lady J.

For some reason, I wasn't afraid of dead people. I was curious about death at a young age.
My first experience with death was at the age of 10 or 11.
It was a girl I knew that was hit by a car while she was riding her bike on Peck Blvd.
I didn't go to her funeral.

Mrs. Gaither allowed me to come in and look at her after she had gotten her dressed.
I remember standing there thinking that she was never going to get up again.
It looked as if she had a wig on with two braids or two ponytails.
There was a lace net over her casket.

As I was standing there wondering where did her voice go when she died?.
I noticed a gnat flying around her face.
I lifted the net and swatted the gnat away from her.
I touched her hand and said goodbye.
The lesson I took from that was to be careful while riding a bike and not to ride in the street.
And that children die too.
She wasn't the only child that I knew who died in my childhood.

CHAPTER 3

A Boy Named King

There once was a Little Boy Named King.
And King liked to run.
King was a little boy that lived on Front Street in the projects, across the street from the Booker T Washington Community Center.

King was deaf and couldn't talk.
He wasn't the only kid that I knew that was deaf.
Janell and Coco were also deaf.
King would go to the center every day if he could.
To run and play with the other kids.

King wore hearing aids and he could only mimic a few words.
King had a way of communicating with people.

One rainy afternoon while running across the street, to or from the community center King was hit by a car.

I didn't see King get hit by the car I came after.
The vision, the memory of him laying in the street, stays with me.

It was a cloudy afternoon.

The sky was a deep blue color. I'll never forget that day because of the rain.

The fire department and the rain helped wash his blood away that was in the street. The Sky was sad that day.

On my way to Grandmother's house, I found out about King.

So the two safe places that I would run to were within 2 blocks of each other off of the main street.

Lady J.

Running from physical abuse.
Taking the mental abuse with me everywhere I went.

In many ways, I feared and loved my mother.

The things she would say to me when she was upset would cut Like a Knife.

Now let me say by no means was I an angel.
I'm pretty sure I did a lot of things as a child growing up to upset my mother.
She had a way of saying things that hurt deep within.

It made me wonder where my father was and think about when my Grandfather would get after my sister and me when we were younger.

He would say "I'm going to set your soul on fire" If you don't stop, whatever it was my sister and I were doing at that time.

Thinking about my soul being on fire was enough for me to know that he was serious.
And my mother was serious as well about the rules in her house. Whenever I would run I wouldn't be gone for long.

CHAPTER 4

Just Like Your Father

From time to time Mother would go on a rant about my Father.

A man that I had never even seen before.

She would say to me "You just like your Father, He ain't s***!
And You ain't going to be s***!

As a child, I didn't understand what it meant but it hurt.

As a Teenager it was confusing.
And it also made me think about this Man that I had never seen before.

This sparked my curiosity.
This was the start, The beginning of my search, my Journey for my father.

And I often thought about how different my life would be if my father was there.

In my daily routine, I would do as much as I could do around the house to help Mother.

Monday through Friday when I got up in the morning, I would get my sisters dressed for school, then I would get myself dressed.

I would make sure everyone's hair was combed and I did the best I could to make sure they made it to school in time for Breakfast.
And then I would go to school.

Most of the time I would be late.

On the days that I made it to school on time, it was like my body was at school but my mind was at home. It would be hard for me to concentrate.

Most of the time I did whatever I had to do just to make it through the day.

Grade School and Junior High School.

I have a lot of memories from school.

Some good, some bad, and some traumatizing.

I made my first real friends at school.

Grade school is where I met my Best friend that would be my best friend for all of my life.

Grade school and Junior High is also where I had bullies. It seems like it was always a girl trying to fight me or a boy doing something mean to me.

I have a vivid memory of being bullied.

Walking home from elementary school it was always a fight.

That's where one of my bullies called me out one day.

She was bigger than me and taller than me and she always wanted to fight somebody.

There were a few girls like that just for no reason.

One morning on the way to school my bully was picking on me and she told me we were going to fight after school.

I can't even remember why she wanted to fight me.

More than likely it was nothing at all.

I came up with my plan before I got to school. I picked up a rock and put it in my pocket.

I had the Rock in my pocket all day ready for after school.

Once school was let out, I took my normal route home.

Once I made it to Garden Avenue and crossed the street to go through the field,

I was taking the shortcut to my grandmother's house. I'm halfway through the field and there she was standing in the middle of the field.

She wasn't alone; she had other kids with her. I was just going to walk by and act as if I didn't see her. When I tried to walk by she stopped me and said that we were about to fight.

I didn't say anything, I stuck my hand in my pocket and held on to the rock that I had in my pocket.

I said to her that I didn't want to fight!

At that point, she hit me first.

I bald up my fist and hit her straight in her mouth with The Rock.

At that time she wasn't my only bully, and I wasn't the only one she bullied; however, it stopped her from messing with me in grade school.

I was bullied so much, in turn, I bullied someone.

Someone that I have since apologized to for my actions.

And then there was my Mother!.

My mother came to my Elementary school, in Grand Fashion, one day.

I was in class and she was upset about something she couldn't find.
When I say Mother was heated!.

The teacher called me in the hallway, I looked at my mother and I knew she was Pissed!.

Mother was standing there and she started yelling at me, and then she slapped me in the face!.

The classroom door was open so the other children heard it. They heard the slap as well as me crying.
I was so embarrassed, I was ashamed.

By the time I made it to Junior High School, I had already begun to shut down.

The Jr High school that I attended was on the other side of town. so every morning we had to take the bus.
Taking the bus to school in the morning.
The kids that went to Jr high school from Projects, made riding the bus fun.
We always had a good laugh in the morning.

Someone would be cracking jokes on another person.
Most mornings it would be Martin Blackson and Raymon Crown going back and forth.

And the Jokes would always be about somebody's mama or the roaches in the projects.
Because the Projects had Roaches.

I had very few friends in Junior high school.
I also felt like an outcast, I didn't fit in.
I felt awkward. From time to time, the other kids would tease me.

Something that started when I was a young child.
Sometimes the girls would be mean to me and they would call me names that hurt my feelings.
Because my hair was short and I was all legs.
Whenever they wanted to hurt my feelings they would say that I looked like a boy.

It bothered me. I had my good days and I had my bad days. and I spent most of my days in school, in In-School suspension, or talking to the counselor.

It was one teacher, in particular, that worked at another school.

Miss Ayers, worked for the city schools and she also lived on the same side of town.

She knew my family and for some reason, I swear this Woman could look at me and tell when something was wrong.

Lady J.

She never asked me about my business or my Mother's business. I just felt comfortable enough to go to her when I wanted to talk.

I would just like to be around her.

She always dressed nicely and her tasteful shoes were like no other.
The conversations that we had were always Encouraging and Motivating.

Miss Ayers always encouraged me to do something.
It didn't matter what it was, Just do something!.
I remember wishing that she was my mother.
I wanted to live with her.
I just had a feeling that my life would have been different.
At that time in my life, any place but home seemed to be better.

CHAPTER 5

Going To School

Junior high was a struggle trying to fit in and maintain what was going on at home.

I never talked to my Mother about school.

I never told her about being bullied.

Afraid to talk to her about the things that girls my age at the time would have talked to their mother about.
We didn't talk about my transition into a young lady in a way that made me feel comfortable. She would talk at me not with me.

Yes, I had a Grandmother and I also had Aunts that I could talk to. However, that was one of the Biggest problems that Mother had with me going to the family and talking to them about things that were going on in her house.

I learned about my menstrual cycle through a friend of the family (Thelma G) she would always talk to me when I was younger.
I could just be walking up the street and she would stop me and talk to me. I will always be grateful to her for our conversations about life.
The fear made me so afraid. I was so afraid that when my breast started developing, I didn't even go to her then to talk to her about the knots that were growing in my chest.

Afraid I'd done something wrong and I would be punished. I was trying to avoid that at all costs. At this point, I can't say if I had any head concussions. I had fractures in my arms.

Bruises and welts all over my body from being hit with sticks and brooms extension cords or whatever she could get her hands on at those times that it would happen.

It didn't happen all of the time

Lady J.

The only time it seemed like I could get away from the house was when I went to school or babysitting.

Mentally I would leave one type of abuse only to have to deal with it at another location.

In the beginning, I liked Jr high school.

Most of the time when I was at school my body would be there but my mind was at home or someplace in the trees.

I was also held back in the 7th grade, behind my friends that I started school with.

In the morning before I could go to school I had to make sure my younger sisters were dressed and on their way to school before I could even leave the house.

I would walk my sisters most of the way and then go to school. The homeroom bell rang before they even had to be at school.

It seemed I was always late and I missed a lot of days.

One day a month I would have to walk across the River, to the west side, to the Unemployment office, to have a green card stamped for Mother to receive her government assistance.

It would be times when Mother had an appointment for recertification.

I would be the one that would meet with the caseworker with a note from Mother.

Each month she would ask me the same questions and each month I would give her the same answer. I knew what and what not to say to her.

Over time you realize some things that you can't say to certain people even if it is the truth.

And an ass-whooping will make you remember that.

I remember one month I had to go for recertification so that meant I had to fill out all of the forms.

And at this time I was just learning how to read and write and missing a lot of days didn't help at all.

So there were a lot of words I hadn't learned at that point.

A lot of the questions were yes or no or fill in the blank.

I will never forget. I came to a question that I didn't know the answer to. So I ask the caseworker what I should put in this space? And she said to me just to write unknown.

I sat there for about a minute after she told me what to write in the space. I sat there thinking and trying to spell the word out of my head because I couldn't spell it.

I remember the caseworker asking me how I was doing in school.

I can't remember what I said as I was fighting in my head trying to spell this word.

I remember spelling it this way (Unnone).
When I finished filling out the forms I handed them back to the caseworker.

She and I went over the paperwork together, one question at a time.
When she came to the question where I wrote unknown, I watched her correct my spelling on the paper, And then she took the pencil and drew a light circle around the world.
The Caseworker turned to me and read the question to me. and we spelled the word out loud together.
And that's how I learned how to spell the word Unknown. " Donna A"

CHAPTER 6

Anxiety from school

School and babysitting were my getaways. and I often learned a lesson or two.

Valuable lessons through both.
The lessons I learned from school weren't always about school work.

I learned a lot about people and character. and I came away with a few good memories. Like the one time, I tried out for cheerleading.

My sister was a cheerleader.
I had never done anything like that and I was very shy however I wanted to try out.

What I now know to be anxiety, was so bad that I asked the judges to hold up a piece of paper over their faces so I could perform.

I look back at that day and I laugh, however it wasn't funny when I was going through it.

Or the time I tried out for the basketball team, I ended up being the ball girl.
My sister was on the team. She made being on the team fun.
My sister is the only girl that I knew at the time that could take a Big Mac and bite it one time and half the sandwich would be gone.
She was a lot of fun. Jr High School is where I met my sister.
I guess it wouldn't be junior high school without the drama.
People fight after school at least once a week. And the rumors that people would spread throughout the school always had something to do with sex it seemed.

I even heard a rumor about myself and the boy at 4th Street Park.
We were at the park, however, it was NO sex involved.

It was always something going on and all I wanted was to go to school and not be bothered.

To be the butt of someone's joke is not a good feeling

I experienced it first hand.

One day at school it was lunchtime.
After we ate we could go to the dance or the movie.
On this particular day, I was standing in line waiting to go to the dance.

A boy walked up behind me and set my hair on fire.
For no reason at all.

Someone standing behind me helped me pat the fire out.
I was embarrassed and humiliated.

After that, the other kids started teasing me and I still had to go to lunch.

I made it through that somehow.
Junior High wasn't all bad for me.
I had good experiences too.

Jr high school is where I met my half-sister. And from that day to this day we have been sisters.
The one I spoke about that was a cheerleader and played basketball.

My mother always told me that I had a half-sister. We didn't meet until Junior High School.
One day at lunch I was standing in line waiting to get my food and someone that I was talking
to asked me within our conversation, "Is that your sister right there". I turned around and looked and
at the same time, she turned around and looked at me.

This is how I was introduced to my Sister.
My Big Sister.
She and I are the same age 4months apart and she is the oldest.

Once I made it home from school that day I told Mother that I met a girl at school.

Someone had introduced us and said that she was my sister.

Mother told me yes you have another sister. And she went on to say "You mark my words your
Father is going to wait until you two are grown and come back to home.
This was the first time she spoke about my father without cursing him that I can remember.

Over time Sister and I started talking when we ran into each other at school.

This would be the beginning of our relationship as sisters and as friends.
I would go across the tracks and visit her from time to time.
I also learned the lady at the store, Miss M, was her Grandmother.

Lady J.

I knew it was something about that lady, that when I went in the store that made me be on my best behavior.

She never saw me do anything wrong. I just feared her in that way. It was the look I saw her give other children when they were in the store acting up or trying to steal something and got caught.

The corner store was the last stop after school.
Dick's on front street.
I would see my sister's grandmother almost every day.

Not too long after that, the Jr high school that I was attending was going to be closing.

The kids that lived in the bottom would be going to school on the Westside.

We were the first blacks students from the Eastside to go to that Junior High school on the westside.
At that time it may have been two black students at that school that lived on the westside.

That in itself was a whole new experience.

A short time after that I was beginning to miss so much school, and my behavior changed for the worst. I was sent to the Alternative school.

It was an old Ice Cream Parlor.
A last-ditch effort at the time to help me get an education.

CHAPTER 7

Kicked Out

So now I'm in a building with the worst of the worst.

The distractions of all the inner-city schools.

Penny Myers, Megan Jones were two that I knew from the hood.

Penny lived down the street from my Grandparents. Megan lived on Grant circle.

Once a week the school would take the students to the YMCA. This is where I stood up to someone that I was being bullied by.

Megan Smith was a white girl who acted Black. Her mother owned a bar named The Island and she dated Black men.
I guess that's where her boldness came from.
I can't remember why we had words, all I remember is she wanted to fight.
At this point, I can say that I was afraid to fight. I had been bullied most of my life by different kids that I grew up with.

So Penny said to me, "The only way people are going to stop fucking with you is when you Fuck somebody up".
I have to be honest, I was scared.

So instead of fighting her, I locked her in the bathroom.
She wanted to fight before we got on the bus.
I waited to use the bathroom last and she came in after me. So when she went into the stall to use it, I waited a minute and walked out.
I noticed that the door had a turn lock on the outside of the door as I was walking out, so I locked it and got on the bus.
All the other students began to get on the bus.
After about ten minutes of waiting the Teacher did a headcount of the students and noticed Megan wasn't on the bus.

Lady J.

She went back into the building to look for her.

When she returned Megan was with her.

Megan was Pissed, to say the least.

Her face was red as a Cayenne pepper!

I'll never forget the look on her face. She was mad as hell and breathing hard and wanted to fight.

And on top of that, the teacher was upset. So now I got this big white girl that wants to fight me, I know I'm going to get kicked out of school and when I get home my mother is straight going off!

After that situation Megan and I became friends.

CHAPTER 8

Last Chance

Alternative school let me know that I wasn't the only one with the problems.

I would be sitting in class looking out the window.

It was a halfway house across the street, that was the first time I ever saw a midget coming out of the house.

One day after school on my way home I saw him. I must have been staring at him because he yelled at me and said, "Stop staring at me"!.

He wasn't the only thing that I was staring at on my way home. It didn't matter which way I took, it was always the scenic route.

Making it home from school was a challenge in itself.

My mother never encouraged me to go to school. That pushes kids' needs from a parent.

I felt like she didn't care.

Over the next few years, things began to change.

I started maturing. developing as a young woman and Mother and I started bumping heads about everything.

I feel like This is when she begins to plant the seed of doubt in me.

I did everything I could as a teenager to try and be what was considered normal.

I had dreams, goals, and aspirations.

That was destroyed by my Mother right along with everything I had already experienced in my life.

Everything I ever wanted to do or Participate in, she made me doubt myself.

It was a mind game to her.

I could be wrong.

It's how I felt at the time.

Lady J.

When I was younger, I went to the community center. I wanted to be a part of everything.

I wanted to be a girl Scout and I only made it to be a brownie. I would participate in the haunted houses and go to as many dances as she would allow me to.

Looking back it seemed I always wanted to be a part of something. I wanted to belong, belong with the group.

For some reason I was always singled out, left behind, excluded without notice.

Every year the Community Center would have a talent show. And I always wanted to win!

I always wanted to be in a group, a winning group.

The closest I ever got to a group was a duet.

And I tried the duet thing twice.

Once I stole a whole book of my mother's food stamps, and I spent the whole day going between Dicks and Dons stores cashing in food stamps to get the change so that I could get an outfit to wear for the talent show.

Myself and my friend Michael.

We performed a modern dance together. We didn't even place third that year.

Michael was my first friend as a boy.

We did a lot of things together.

The final time that I participated in the talent show was with my Uncle Martin.

My performance was modern dance again and my uncle played the saxophone and sang a song as I danced.

The song that he performed was titled "Too Hot by Kool & The Gang".

In the beginning, when I had the idea about being in the talent show I asked one of my friend's girls to be in it with me and she agreed.

But somehow when it was time for the show she didn't want to be in it with me so I had to dance alone.

My feelings were hurt and I was afraid to dance alone.

Maybe I didn't dance well enough for her to dance with me.

Once the announcer called our names it was Showtime!.

When my uncle began to sing the words to the song, " At 17 we fell in love. High School sweethearts love was so brand new".

As I began to dance Something came over me. And once he began to play the saxophone it made the memory for me something that I will never forget.

I had made my mind up before the show that I was never going to be in the talent show again.

It was always hard for me to find someone that wanted to participate with me as a team and I was tired of losing, and all I wanted to do was win once.

Every year it seemed like the same three or four people would win the talent show.

Yes, They were all good performances, however, I felt as if other acts deserved a chance to win also.

By the end of our performance, I realized that I wasn't alone because I was with my Uncle.

At the end of the show, the judges tallied up the votes. They had all of the performers come in front of the crowd and stand as they called the names. In my mind, I already knew we didn't win because I never won anything!.

Once they thanked everyone for participating in the talent show and announced the winners.

The judges started with the third-place winner.

I didn't hear our names and I was ready to go. I had already accepted defeat, at least I didn't give up.

Then they announced the second place winners and called our names!.

When I tell you I was so happy, you would have thought we won first place.

I'm more than sure that we won second place because of my uncle's talents.

He could always sing and play the saxophone; he was musically inclined that way. That was the last time I was ever in the talent show.

I only wanted to win once and it didn't matter what place. And second place was good enough for me.

CHAPTER 9

Miss Black Hamilton

I learned about the pageant through a friend. It was a pageant for girls my age, Black girls. I signed up for the pageant before I even asked my mother about it. I was excited.

When I went home and talked to her about it, from that point on She created the doubt that I had in myself. She told me that I could not be in the pageant.

In my mind I was already preparing little did she know.

So over the next few weeks, I would sneak to the Rehearsals. I would go anyway even though I didn't have what I needed.

And I think a few of the girls knew it. I could tell by the way they treated me. Being mean and making jokes about me. It was a girl that I was friends with named "Tish".

"Tish" and I became friends in grade school. She lived on Grant circle.

Once we began Junior High School we went to different schools.

Over the next few weeks, I learned the song that I wanted to perform. The next thing I had to figure out was what I was going to wear.

Now Mother had a lot of clothes and all the newest things that were out of the latest fashions.

I would sneak into Mother's room when she left the house to look through her clothes, trying to find something to wear for the pageant.

When I told her that I was still going to be in the pageant and that I needed something to wear.

My Mother told me that I couldn't wear any of her things.

So now I had to find something to wear and someone to fix my hair.

My hair was always short and I had a complex about that.

I saved a few dollars that I earned from babysitting to buy Revlon perm from Revco on High street.

After I got the perm I made an appointment with a Beautician that I knew of by the name of "B Black".

She worked at the Les More Hair Studio.

Located on the corner of Second & Walnut Street. Gleaves Barbershop was on the other side.

I talked to "Miss B" about fixing my Hair for the pageant.

She told me to come back the morning of the pageant. Now to find something to wear to the Pageant.

I went to visit Two Sisters, they lived on 2nd Street.

This is one of the places I could go when I was allowed to go out of the house.

Always Fashionable and they also made their clothes. Now and then my mother would let me spend the night on the weekends.

We would stay up most of the night listening to music, watching TV, and eating.

"Miss H", made the best barbecue and collard greens, The Best Soul Food.

I went to my friend "V" and asked her if she had something that I could wear. "V" also had her own money.

She was injured in the corner store.

The owner's son was nailing a piece of wood and the nail hit her in the eye.

Her Sister "C" had Good Taste in clothing and Shoes.

By the end of the visit, they had got me together.

I had what I needed for the pageant.

I had to hide the clothes from my mother because she said I couldn't be in the pageant.

The next few weeks were kind of smooth.

I was able to keep my mother happy by doing what I needed to do. Then I would go to practice and come home without her even knowing.

The Saturday morning of the pageant, I got up and went to get my hair fixed.

I was nervous about getting my hair fixed and I was even more worried about my mother catching me trying to sneak out of the house.

It was my 1st time going to the beauty salon. And I always wanted to go.

There would be times that I had to go to Don's store for my Mother and I would walk that way.

And I would say to myself, "One day I'm going to go there to have my hair fixed".

I always wanted my hair Finger Waved.

So now I'm at the Salon.

I told "Miss B" how I would like to have my hair fixed. And let me tell you that she was The Best at Finger waves.

I went from a "TWA" (Teeny Weeny Afro) to a Relaxed Finger wave. I was very excited. From the shampoo bowl to her styling chair I was feeling better about myself.

Fear of the unknown began to set in.

Not knowing if I'm going to look right.

I never had my hair like this before so I was very nervous.

She wouldn't let me look at my hair until she was finished.

And what I mean by finished is, That final spin in the hair chair with finishing sprays of Hair spray and Oil sheen.

She handed me a hand mirror to see my face with my back towards the Big mirror so that I could see the back first.

When "Miss B" turned me around in the chair to see myself for the first time with my hair fixed, It was the First time that I felt Pretty.

The First time that I felt like A Girl.

My Hair Permed Fried and Waved to the side. Pretty!.

I didn't look like a BOY! By the time I made it back home, it was time for me to go to the Pageant.

As I was about to leave the house to go uptown to meet the other girls at The Moose Hall,

As I was trying to sneak out.

I thought she was asleep. I was about to go out the back door when my mother called me back into the house. I'm thinking to myself, she's not going to let me go.

I went back to see what she wanted.

My mother handed me a Garment bag.

I was confused but I was also Happy.

I had been in my mother's closet trying on clothes and shoes putting together outfits that I wanted to wear and I think she knew that.

And She gave them to me at the last minute.

I was in the pageant.

My Talent was singing and I couldn't sing, so I lip-synced to a song called "Call Me" by Skyy.

I didn't win, I didn't even place.

But this was the first time that I was in a Beauty Pageant.

Not only a beauty pageant, The 1ˢᵗ Miss Black Hamilton pageant".

It was something that I felt that I could do and it Excited me and made me forget about everything that I was going through.

This was when I realized I wanted to be someone.

CHAPTER 10

Our One And Only

I can't tell you how it happened or when it happened. All I know is that He was there.

This would be The Man that would change my mother's life, change our lives.

Everything is Beautiful in the beginning, like the Soft and Sweet smell of the candles and incense that my Mother would burn in the evenings.

Mother met a New Man.

This man would change her life.

"KB" He would come at night and often. And with this Man DRAMA came with it. And when I say drama, I mean drama on a whole different level!.

Something that seemed common growing up, he had another woman.

A woman that he had been with for some years and he lived with her also.

Now over the next few years, my mother and this man developed a real relationship. And from the relationship, my Brother was conceived.

My Only Brother. This is where our life was turned into a lifetime movie.

When other people learned that my mother was pregnant and that she was seeing this man, the other woman found out.

Keep in mind, I'm a mother's oldest child and I'm seeing all of this.

At this time The other Woman began to stalk my mother.

I mean to the point that she would visit people that lived around us in the housing complex.

She would be across the street one day and next door the next.

She was good at setting up the scenario to create drama for my mother with other women as well.

And the thing was, I wasn't afraid of her.

I said to my mother a couple of times let me fight her! It was just that bad.

It got so bad that she even faked being pregnant so that she would be pregnant at the same time.

She would dress up in maternity clothes and put a pillow in the front of her pants. And would walk around like that.

The thing I didn't understand was, why no one ever said anything to her about that.

It seemed bizarre to me, almost crazy. This woman was delusional and obsessed with my mother being pregnant.

Every other week she was setting up a way to have communications with my mother.

Lady J.

I could be walking to the store or coming home from school and I would see this lady close to our house.

She would call the police and make false reports.

She made calls to cps.

When I say this woman was "Treacherous"!.

It was so bad that it was said that this woman was digging holes in her backyard and burying pictures of my family for whatever reason.

I thank Jehovah, that my mother and my Grandmother always had us protected in prayer.

It didn't stop "KB" from seeing my Mother.

It seems as if once the other woman found out about Baby, he began to come around my mother even more.

He would come on his lunch break, all through the week and weekends. And this made my Mother Happy. And we were happy.

She gave me more freedom, time away from the house. I made a few friends at school so when I could go out I would visit.

I would go to the east side of town and spend time with my sister. I was able to visit a lot of my friends.

This summer I even found out where my other Grandparents lived.

CHAPTER 11

Looking For Daddy

By the end of that summer, I began my journey looking for my father. I knew his name and where his parents lived on 12th street.

The crazy thing about that was, the people that would be My Grandparents lived a half of a block from the Jr high school that I attended.

I would walk by the house hoping to get a glance at my Father. Hoping to get a glance at Someone.

One afternoon, after school as I walked past the house.

I saw an old man standing in the backyard. I walked around the back of the house and spoke to him.

Right away He started talking to me as if he knew who I was. Overtimewish,t least once a week I would stop and talk to him. This man would be my Grandfather, "GrandDad", "Decon G".

Over time he initiated the conversation about my father. He would Indirectly give me details about my father and his whereabouts. and what my father was doing with his Life.

However, he never gave me the phone number.

For a while, I kept it to myself and I never told Mother that I had been to the house.

I never told her that I talked to the Man that I thought was my Grandfather.

In the past Mother expressed herself about The Family and it wasn't a good thing.

Mother would have her moments and she would Express Herself loud and clear!

I don't know if it seemed as if, Whenever I did something wrong or we weren't Seeing eye to eye, that's when I would hear it.

The one thing she would say was, You're just like your Father.

He ain't s*** and you ain't going to be s***!. I was confused because I never even remember seeing this man so how would I know that he wasn't s***and at this time I'm 16 years old.

All I know is when she said it, my feelings would be hurt. From time to time mother would talk about him.

She would always say he's going to come back when you're grown and don't have to pay child support.

I often thought about if I would ever see him, what kind of man he was, what he even looked like.

In my mind, I had an Imaginary Father.

I made him the way I wanted him to be.

I made him Tall and Handsome and in my mind very nice to me. The type of Father that would love his child.

This began my search for him.

After the fact, things started happening for all the right reasons I could say.

The way I would meet what would be my family on my father's side.

One day I was in the store and a lady walked up to me.

A Tall dark skinned slim nicely dressed woman wearing glasses.

She said hello and introduced herself to me. She called me by my name and I had no clue who this woman was.

She said to me, I'm your Aunt Lorraine, I'm your Father's Sister. Your Father is My Only Brother.

From that day forward I began to spend time with my Aunt at her house and I had a chance to meet my cousins. I have a lot of cousins.

McGlen Street is where she lived.

And right behind her house was a train track.

I love this house. the way the house was designed on the inside.

Where the children slept it was two ways upstairs, the left side of the stairs was where the boys slept and on the right side was where a girl slept, and maybe the other way around I can't remember it's been so long.

In the morning when I spent the night, My Aunt would be up making Breakfast.

It would still be dark outside but the smell of the sausage and the bacon cooking woke me up every time.

I would go down to the kitchen and watch her cook, Everything was homemade. She would make these Homemade Buttermilk biscuits.

Once she mixed all the ingredients I think the magic came in when she patted the biscuit together.

She would make it like a ball and pat it out into the shape of a biscuit, and when they were done she would put Real Butter on top.

On the plate with the sausage and the eggs and grits then she would pour some syrup out of a can that came from Georgia.

The Best Southern Breakfast I ever had.

She would share little things about my father, bits and pieces. She told me his full name and that he lives in California.

For the next three years, I ran my Grandmother's phone bill up to at least $600 a month, trying to locate this man.

I called every number that the directory would give me for any man that had the same name as my Father.

I didn't realize at the time how big California was.

It was like looking for a needle in a Haystack.

28

And then one day I Found That Needle.

As the phone was ringing I was contemplating what I was going to say to him.
I didn't know if I had the right number or if it was another miss.
The phone rang a few times and then a woman answered and I asked to speak to AW.

The woman said, yes hold on and she called him on the phone.

When He answered the phone, I told him who I was and he was speechless.
He didn't even know what to say to me, so I began to talk to him.

I began to talk to him as if we talked all the time as if he was a part of my life daily.

He didn't say much but yes and ok and at the end of the conversation I said, ``I love you Daddy and his reply was "okay".
That's all he said was yes and okay.
We went on this way for a couple of years.

CHAPTER 12

The Picture On The Wall

The first time I saw my other Grandmother.
I was afraid to Knock on the door.

It was Father's Day and I baked a cake for my Grandfather and I had a card for him.

Opening the gate to walk into the yard was the hardest thing for me.
Once I made it to the door I was so nervous!
I was so nervous that when I knocked on the door, I set the Cake and the Card down on the table that was sitting on the porch, And I ran out of the yard.

The next time I went to visit, I was with my Half-sister.
I'll never forget it!

She knocked on the door and Another one of my Father's sisters answered the door.
As we were walking in, My Aunt spoke to my sister, and then She looked at me and rolled her eyes as she walked away.

I heard her once she walked into the kitchen and asked the question who I was, therefore.

At that time my Grandmother was walking into the living room. At the same time, I'm looking around the room at the pictures on the walls.
It was one picture of a Young Man in a yellow shirt.
I never asked who it was and my Grandmother never Bothered to tell me.
I mean at this point she never said she was my grandmother.
I just happened to go inside the house with my sister.
I wasn't invited. My sister took me with her one day after school and I never thought to ask my sister who was in the picture.

After that visit, I could tell that my sister was The Chosen One.
It also made my visits past the house far fewer and in between.

My Feelings were hurt and I could tell the difference in the way they treated me as opposed to the way they treated my sister at that time.

After that day I started spending more time with my sister. And because of her, I met the woman who is said to be my Grandmother and an Aunt, and I still haven't met my Father yet.

That would soon change.

CHAPTER 13

Good And Bad News.

My Mother got Good news that we were going to be moving.
No, we weren't moving into a house, we were moving into a bigger apartment in the projects.
Vidourek, Drive.

A street that I was far too familiar with wasn't the first time I lived on Vidourek, drive and it wasn't going to be the last.

We had a couple of months before the apartment would be ready for us to move in. It was on the other end of the projects, on the backside by the river.

Living on Walnut drive it's like being in the front of a battle zone.
Right off of Front Street.
Everyone that came to the projects had to pass by our house to come into the complex.
Now we would be in the back a little ducked off but right in the middle of everything. To leave out of the complex, you would have to drive by our new home.

Sometimes it's better to see people go than come.
It was more kids on the other side too.
And my Godmother Anna lived across the street.

CHAPTER 14

He Is The Father

November 1st The baby was born.

At this time there were no sonograms where you could tell the birth of the baby. You would have to wait until the baby was born and it was a big surprise.
This time it was a boy!.

Out of four girls, my mother finally was blessed with her Son, her Only Son!
And for me, It was one of the happiest days of my life.
To have a Little Brother he was my everything.
After his birth, everyone was focused on the baby.
There would be days that I couldn't wait to get home from school to play with my brother.

When he was born I told all of my friends about him and I would show the baby picture to everyone that would look at him.

A couple of times my mother even let my friends come into the house to look at him.
I remember one day I came home from school so excited to see the baby.

As I walked up to his bassinet and leaned over to pick him up the legs collapsed on the bassinet on one end.

I grabbed my brother up out of the bassinet so quickly and kicked the leg out on the bottom so that it didn't fall.
If that bassinet had hit the floor and my brother had been in it, my mother would have killed me.
I can still feel the way my heart was beating at that time. I love my brother!.

Now the thing about my brother being born, I had never seen so much drama about a baby before.
It was like my brother was a famous person's baby.
A lot of talk about him and who his father was.
As it seemed that things were getting better, my Mother was hit with another blow a year later.
My sister was pregnant.

Lady J.

My sister was two years younger than I.

A baby having a baby, and at that time it was only a couple of girls that I knew of that had a baby that young, teenage pregnancy.

Our Mother was not happy about it at all.

When I look back at it, I remember a conversation that she had with us in the bathroom.

Just out of the blue she called us into the bathroom. I think maybe she may have been taking a bath.

My mother must have sensed the change in my sister and me.

I remember standing at the door and she was asking us about having sex.

At that point, I hadn't even had sex yet, only a little kissing and touching.

Mom was talking to us about getting on birth control. She asked us if we wanted to get on birth control. I said yes and my sister told her no, that she didn't want birth control to mess up her body. I don't think we spoke about sex too much after that.

And the next thing you know, my sister is pregnant.

CHAPTER 15

The Fall

It's starting to get dark earlier so I had to be home earlier.

Trying to make curfew was sometimes hard to do.

It was always something with my mother when it came to us being home on time.

And I had a few nights where I came home late and it was worth it!.

Getting hit or grounded, because at that time she was still hitting me. I did the best I could to follow the rules in her house.

I was also getting older and beginning to have a voice for myself. I wouldn't say so much that I was talking back, or being disrespectful.

I knew right from wrong.

My punishment was always severe.

I would try to talk myself out of an ass whooping!.

If I did something wrong, let me explain to you why I did it. I never got any further than, "mama let me tell you something" right before the beating began.

The beatings weren't as bad as when I was younger and it wasn't as many. however when it did occur it was really bad and at 16 it was too much.

I don't think it was so much the physical abuse, it was the verbal abuse.

That's what hurts the most.

The physical abuse after a while, I learned how to dodge her and get away from her.

But her words, it was nowhere for me to run to.

Her words followed me everywhere I went.

I guess I could say I feared her so much that, mentally I took her everywhere I went.

I guess on the outside looking in, it would look as if I was disrespecting and fighting with my mother when I was only defending myself.

Trying to stop her from hurting me. I loved and feared my mother. I know I ran away a few times or attempted to run away.

It was something about being out that late at night.

Not knowing where I was going to sleep. Hungry, scared not knowing what to do, that didn't sit right with me.

So I always ended up back at home. I mean I knew a couple of girls that would run away from home.

On the inside looking out, it always seemed as if those girls were having fun.

Doing what they wanted to do.

Acting as if they were grown. On the other hand, it was very scary to me.

So when I put myself in a situation and I was out late, the anxiety of trying to get back home I still feel it today. Just thinking about it.

Being out at night at a young age was like being in the belly of the beast.

You see things you're not supposed to see and it's always someone there to take advantage of you.

One night I was walking home and a woman that I knew walked up to me.

She said to me that she had a picture of me.

She wanted me to go to her house so she could give it to me.

The lady went into the house and got the picture and came out and handed it to me.

She asked me is this you?".

I looked at the picture and it was a picture of a girl my age naked laying on a mattress with whipped cream on her private part.

First of all, I had never taken a naked picture before. And second, why would she think it was me?.

Once I told her no! Her reply was I thought it was you.

That's how it is living in the hood!.

The rumors.

If she thought it was me I'm sure she said it to other people that she showed the picture to.

And no telling who she got the picture from.

All I know is that it wasn't me!.

Looking back when I would run away it wasn't to be with boys or to drink alcohol, or do drugs.

I would be late for curfew and I figured I might as well stay out, I'm going to get beat anyway.

Even if it was just an hour late.

The punishment will be far too severe.

I wanted to get out of her house.

That was always my thought until I was out there in the streets.

Then all I wanted to do was go home.

Everything my grandparents and my mother warned me about that would be out there in the streets was out there.

At different times I would see those things that they spoke about.

So I did have a sense of fear when it came to certain things in the streets.

When I say peer pressure at its best, I mean that.

CHAPTER 16

1981

Valentine's Day 1981 my whole world would be shaken up.
Standing in the yard about 6:30 or 7:00 in the evening it was dark out.

I saw my grandmother's car turning into the projects off of Front street.

My Grandfather had been sick for a while battling cancer and they took him to the hospital.

I thought everything would be all right and he would be coming back home.
When I saw my grandmother's car turn the corner I just knew, I just knew that my Grandfather was gone.

I remember screaming and I jumped up and down for a minute, I was crying.
When my mother got out of the car she said to me, Daddy died.
I know now that it did something to me.
It changed my life.
It changed my life to the point that I began to rebel, rebel against myself after the fact.

Things started happening in my life.
And for my Mother, it was another level of trauma that she had to deal with, because of the relationship that she had with her Father.

When my Grandfather died, The whole family's life changed. I thought about a lot of things, the first thing I thought about was who was going to protect me?.

I would always run to my Grandfather when something would happen and he would always make it right in the way that he did.
I even wondered why he had to die because I needed him.

My Grandfather was the first person in my family that I knew died. And as a child, I always had a curiosity about death so now it's my Grandfather.

Lady J.

I kept saying I don't want to go to the funeral. but I knew as the oldest grandchild we all had to go.

At this time it was a two-day service.
They would have the wake on One Day and then the funeral of the next day.

I had a relationship with Mrs.G so I could always go to the funeral home whenever I wanted to.
It was just something that I did. I would visit her and talk to her or go to the store for her.

Or just sit on the steps at the funeral home.

Now it's my turn to go to the funeral home and do what I see all the other sad people do.
I used to wonder why they would cry when they would come out now I'm about to find out.
The morning of the wake I got up and I walked to the funeral home. Mrs.G let me come in.
At this time she had my Grandfather already prepared for the funeral.

At G's funeral home, once you walk in that front door you make that slight right, that's where the body would be.

As I walked in I looked to the right and I could see my Grandfather's head from the doorway.
At this time his head was bald because of cancer.
I think my Uncle Brock cut his hair off once the chemo started making his hair fall out.

I walked over to the room where my Grandfather's body was lying. as I walked up to the casket I was nervous and crying at the same time.
Mrs.G left me there and she went into another part of the funeral home after making sure I was okay.

So now I'm standing there looking at my Grandfather. I rubbed his head and I touched his nose.
I stood there and rubbed his hand for a few minutes.
Grandpa had a couple of fingers that were missing from one hand and that's the hand that I was rubbing.
That was the hand that I would rub when he would talk to me at the house.
In the kitchen that's where the conversations would be at the kitchen table.
I was very sad that morning.
I said goodbye to him and then I went home.
Walking home my thoughts were, how do you say goodbye to someone that can't say it back?.
The wake was in the evening from 6:30 to 8:00-8:30. I remember my mother taking us to the funeral home.
Everyone was crying and sad.
That evening was one of the few times I've ever seen my Grandmother cry.

The next morning when I got up I decided I didn't want to go to the funeral.

I stayed at my grandparent's house and watched all the little kids in the babies.

The only good thing that came out of my Grandfather's death was his Oldest Son coming back home.

At that point the last time I remember seeing Uncle W, I had to be about 10 years old and he was the DJ on the square.

Uncle had moved away to Cleveland Ohio.
After the funeral, he stayed to look after my grandmother.

After my Grandfather's passing, it took about a month or so for things to seem a little normal.

I realized that when someone dies it only takes about 2 weeks of Slow Singing And Flower Bringing and people have to get back to their normal routine in life.

CHAPTER 17

A New House

The wait to move took longer than expected.
We couldn't move until the spring.

Before we moved my sister had the baby.
It was a boy! K.S.S is the birth name that was given to him by my mother.

Mother named him after her brother who died as a baby and Satchel Paige the Baseball player.

Now my sister has a baby.

I would go into her room and look at him. He was a funny-looking baby, he had a Bighead and big eyes.

And he cried all the time.
He was a very sick baby at the beginning of his life.

One day my sister was bathing the baby and he started crying.
And blood started coming out of his tear ducts instead of clear tears.
I went and got Mom and she called 911 and took the baby to the hospital. when Mom left with the baby sister and I was standing at the door as they left.

I remember saying to my sister, ``Do you want to go to the hospital too? That's your baby? She said yes, so we walked over to her sister's Aunt Annie Ruth's house.

Aunt Annie Ruth was sister's Father's Aunt and she lived across the street.
She was a very tall woman with beautiful brown skin.
She reminded me of an Indian with a few open-faced gold teeth. and her hair always looks like she just left the beauty salon.

When she spoke you heard her!.

We walked over to her house to let her know what was going on with the baby and she called a cab, so that sister could go to the hospital too, to be with her baby.

Taking care of her baby wasn't easy either. It seemed like there was always something wrong with him.

When she would feed him, 5 minutes later he would throw up. so that meant she had to change his clothes all the time.

As my nephew got older he required more.
That's where the problem came in with my mother.
The welfare was sending money for my nephew but my mother would keep the money.
My sister and my mother would get into bad arguments and fights about it.

One day, my sister left with her baby and when she returned home, we were sitting in the bedroom.
She pulled out all of this brand-new stuff for the baby.
And I said to her, you're going to get in trouble. She said to me my son will never want for anything!.
And if I have to steal it he will have it.
And she meant that in every essence of the word.
The baby had everything!.
And he had it in every color!.

He even had a top-of-the-line stroller.
In the 80s there was no one pushing $300 strollers in Hood until they learned how to steal them also.
After a while, I'm pretty sure my mother noticed.
And even said something to her about it.
So the Baby was providing for her baby by all means necessary.

CHAPTER 18

Time on my hands

Time away from the house without my sisters.

My mother even started to let me go to parties.

The Pharaohs would give a house party on the weekends. or it would be a party at the community center or the game room.

I didn't get to go to all the parties, but I went enough to get in trouble.

This is how I would meet "R".

"R" was tall, light-skinned, and Handsome.

He lived in the NPA. He wasn't my boyfriend or anything like that, he was just a boy that I knew.

At the time R was dating a couple of girls also.

I would go to his mother's house and be with him whenever I wanted to.

And maybe we got together at a time when he had broken up with one of the other girls.

It didn't matter.

We had no title at that time, we were Friends.

And he wasn't my only friend-boy.

And then there was "D".

D was considered a pretty boy.

He was very popular with the girl's handsome young man.

I met D at the game room on Central Avenue, "We's".

and the thing about it, out of all the girls in the game room, he wanted to talk to me.

D had friends that he hung out with.

They played basketball together almost every day. It was always a game somewhere.

And they always had a place to hang out.

After some time, D took me to hang out with him and his friends.

Jefferson and Cater. Jefferson was allowed to have company in the Basement.

The spot they called "Jamaica".

This is where they would get together and drink beer and do whatever they did.

We would sit and talk while they drank beer. I wasn't drinking at the time. So for a while, we would just talk.

One night D took me home or should I say close to home. Once we made it to the drop-off spot he turned the car off.

We talked for a minute and this was the first time that he kissed me.

This was the first time that I had kissed since Robert kissed me.

And after that first kiss, all I could think about was D.

I started spending less time with my friends and I would spend more time with D when he wasn't working or spending time with other girls.

I have to be honest, D was very Attractive.

He was a very popular young man.

High School Star Basketball player.

He was good at his game. And he looked good doing it!.

After months of seeing each other, D and I had a set date and time that we would get together.

Outside of being spontaneous we would always get together every 1st Sunday of the month.

Every first Sunday of the month his parents would be at church all day.

Morning and afternoon service.

I can honestly say that D was my 1st real sexual experience.

He was the first guy that I took all of my clothes off in front of.

When you're young you're shy about taking off your clothes in front of someone.

I didn't know what I was doing.

I was mimicking what I thought I should do.

And he was there to teach me.

Now when it came to my relationship with R, there was no courtship.

I don't even think I liked him like that.

I was at a Pharaoh party on Fourth street one weekend and somehow we ended up together. That's how it started.

It was nothing like my relationship with D.

When I was with D, I was with D.

When I was with R, I was with R.

Never at the same time.

For the next few months, I would go between the two. That's when I could get out of the house.

CHAPTER 19

Moving

Now the house is packed and we're moving.
I was happy that we were moving and my Mother had a lot of stuff.
And she was very particular about her setup.
My mother always made sure that we had a Beautiful Clean home. so we had a lot of work to do.
I was going to miss the old house, and I had a few good and bad memories from living there.

Like the time a friend of my mother's had her baby at our house and in my mother's bed.

That year, Roger's song More Bounce To The Once, came out.

And when I tell you my mother put a speaker in the front window in the living room, and More Bounce played out of that speaker for 24 hours straight if not more.

If you didn't know, now You know.

My Mother Loved Rodger and so did the rest of the city of Hamilton Ohio!

Or the year we had a bad Rainstorm and there was a blackout in the city.
The storm was so bad that it uprooted a few Big trees in the 2nd ward and Lightning struck the Cross on top of the Catholic Church.
I never realized how big that cross was until I saw it laying on the side of the roof of the church.
After the Storms, we would walk around the neighborhood and look at the damage.

Living in the projects on days like that made it fun.
The friends that I had around the corner I could still see them, it was just around the corner.
The excitement about moving for me was the fact that I was going to have a room to myself.

Something that I didn't have at the old house even though I was the oldest, and that's even before my Sister had the baby.
We moved from three bedrooms and one bath to a four-bedroom and one and a half bath.
Front and back yard, and side yard.

The apartment had three bedrooms upstairs and one downstairs.
The living room had three windows, two in the front, with a side window.

Moving for me was like we were starting all over.
We moved away from all of the old memories and that apartment.

It didn't last long.
My mother's stalker followed us around the corner and up the street.

Once the move was complete and Mom had the house arranged the way she wanted it, My Mother seemed to be in a better place mentally.

Shiny floors and beautiful plants.
Wicker chairs with lights that you could see from the street at night if you were passing by our apartment.

I had my room and my sister and Keith had their room. Little Sister and Baby sister had a room together and my brother slept with my mother.
I chose the bedroom over the living room. The view outside of my bedroom window was the main street and the front yard.
I could also see the highway from my bedroom.
That also meant that if I was looking out of the window I could see everyone that was leaving the complex. That's if they took the back street.
One way in and a few ways out.
In the back of our apartment, was a little Park.
And that's actually what it was called, The little park.
Everything was made for toddlers and little kids, and it had two benches.
The park sat next to the highway that fenced off.
On the other side of the highway is the Great Miami River.
In the spring and summer, you can see people down by the river fishing.

It was a white man and his son Donald, they live in the projects by our old apartment.
I would see them walking through the projects carrying their fishing equipment from the river.
The father would always bring back fish, my mother said you can't eat that fish out the river.
I think it was only 3 White families that lived in the projects at that time.

I would talk to Donald when I would see him outside playing by himself.
He may have been the age of my Little sister.
He had a learning disability and I never saw his mother.
One day someone robbed his father and killed him over Donald's medication that he had to take for his disability.

It was always something strange like that going on. Surrounding drugs.
Drugs made people act crazy and do crazy things. You witnessed a lot of that living in the projects.

Lady J.

Coming home from school was my time to see it all.

I would get off at the first bus stop just to be able to walk down Walnut Street to Front Street through the projects.

If it was something for me to see I was going to see it on my way home from school.

I remember getting off the bus one day and my mother's stalker was standing across the street from the bus stop. We hadn't been in a new apartment that long.

I'm pretty sure she followed me home and our house wasn't hard to find.

CHAPTER 20

Making My Bed Hard

Going to school and babysitting was all I was allowed to do. I had times when I could leave the house but for the majority, I was home.

When I did have the time alone I did what a curious young girl my age would do.

I would spend time with my friends when I could hang out.

I spent a lot of time in my room listening to music and reading magazines.

My mother loved music and most of my life my grandparents always had a piano in the dining room.

Music was my escape.

Billie Holiday, Whitney Houston, Luther Vandross, Roberta Flack, Diana Ross, Roger Troutman, Peabo Bryson, Rufus and Chaka Khan, Frankie Beverly, and maze, Najee, Renee and Angela, Evelyn Champagne King, Phyllis Hyman, Donny Hathaway, Temptations, Michael Jackson, in no particular order, just to name a few.

I love to listen to the radio at night. WDAO was a radio station located in the city of Dayton Ohio. It played all the Urban music. And at night they played Mellow Moods.

My way of escaping.

Saturday nights I would stay up all night and watch TV until the lines would run across the screen, to the end of the broadcast when they showed the American flag about 2:30 in the morning.

Showtime at the Apollo and SNL were my favorite shows. Back in the day when Steve Harvey had hair.

Some weekends I was allowed to go out and some weekends I snuck out.

Monday through Friday it was school!

I would come home from school and go to sleep.

I would come home and go to sleep so much to the point that my mother would keep me up.

She would find something for me to do.
And then one day she asked me" are you pregnant?".

I answered her "no" and I was on the birth control pill.

After about a month of that, the reality was, I was pregnant and on birth control.

I Messed up taking my pills. This is where I feel my relationship with my mother began to change for the worse.

I'm 17 and I'm pregnant living in my mother's house and my sister has just had a baby.
And the same year my half-sister baby, a baby boy.

I was babysitting for other people as much as I could just to be out of my mother's sight. everything that I did, she would get on me about it.

If I slept too much, if I ate too much, it was a problem.
Even at 17 and pregnant I still had to ask permission to do things, go places.
One place I was allowed to go was to walk and visit my sister across the tracks.
I would walk to East avenue and we would sit out on the step and talk or go in her room.
On this particular day as I was walking across the tracks to my Sister's house.
I was at the corner of Walnut and Central Avenue.
As I was crossing the street I happened to look over and make eye contact with a man.
At that very moment, I could not walk, my feet felt as if they were stuck to the ground.
We made eye contact at the same time. I was frozen.
I can't explain what came over my body.
All I know is that I couldn't move for a few seconds.

I continued on my way to my Sister's house. A few hours later she and I were sitting in front of her house on the steps.

A car pulled up and a man got out.
The man got out of his car and walked up to the house. He spoke to my sister and then he went into the house.

A few minutes later my sister was called into the house and I went home.
I told my mother as soon as I went into the house, I think I just saw my Father.

She asked me to describe him to her.
Once I described him, Mother replied "Yes that's that N****!".
And the sad part about that is, He never said one word to me.
Over the next week or so I stayed home. I didn't go visit my sister or my grandparents.

My mother was told that my father was in town for a couple of weeks.

I didn't go across the tracks until after he was gone, But we had a chance meeting.

I was leaving my Aunt Ellie's house, my Mother's sister. as I was walking down the street and A Man came out of nowhere.

He said excuse me, can I talk to you for a minute?.

So I stopped.

I'm looking at this Man from Head to Toe. I'm looking at everything on his body. My heart is beating so fast I thought I was going to Faint!

I didn't know what He was about to say or maybe it was What I wanted him to say. What I've been wanting to hear. as I'm looking at this man's face, I'm noticing that

Our features are the same.

The words that came out of his mouth Shattered my Heart! He said to me,
"Your Mother has been misleading you, I'm Not Your Father".

I stood there for a second, in shock.

I couldn't even speak.

I looked up at him with tears in my eyes and I turned around and walked away with my head down.

I remember walking the whole way home with my head down.

I was almost hit by a car so I had to look up as the tears rolled down my face…

Even though I had never met my father, I never heard of another man's name that was supposed to be my father.

So now I'm tripping in my head. And not only that I'm pregnant.

I knew in my heart that he was my father.

This is what started my downhill spiral, along with all the drama that was about to unfold in my life.

And most if not all of the drama I had to deal with by myself.

My mother set up the appointment for me to go to the clinic, Planned Parenthood to have a pregnancy test and prenatal care.

Now that I had a positive pregnancy test, I had to go and talk to the father.

I knew who the father of my child was, and when I told my mother she didn't believe me. When I went to speak to the father of my child, R, he didn't deny the fact that the baby was his at that time.

The problem only came in after the ex-girlfriend or girlfriend, whatever she was at the time found out.

That's when the rumors started!.

I guess her little feelings were hurt!

And at that time she was running around telling everyone she was a virgin and that she knew for a fact that Reggie wore a condom with me.

As if she was in the room holding the light, or should I say holding my legs!.

I pretty much spent 60% of the pregnancy alone without the baby's father after all of the rumors got started.

I'll say he was there 20% at the beginning and 20% in the end.

By the time I gave birth to my son, his Father seemed to come around a little.

I don't know what he was telling everyone else, However, he never denied it to my face. The birth of the baby was a whole different story.

At this point, my mother was still mad at me and I knew it.

When my contractions started, I was staying with my Grandmother.

I was staying at her house because she went out of town to London Ohio, for a convention for the Jehovah witnesses, something she did every year.

My labor pains started.

I called my mother on the phone to let her know.

My mother told me to call my aunt.

Once I got my Aunt on the phone she told me to wake my Uncle Allen up and to walk to her house.

I woke Uncle up and we began to walk. Every seven steps it seemed, I had a contraction.

Sharp pain to the point that I was bent over.

We walked 6 blocks.

We made it to the house and my Aunt took me to the hospital.

Not only did she take me to the hospital, but she also took me to the hospital and dropped me off.

Dropped me at the emergency entrance and told me to walk into the hospital.

Once again I had that feeling of being alone.

The whole time that I was in labor I was expecting my mother to come to the hospital.

The father of my child was in jail at the time for beating up a white boy.

So I gave birth to my son alone.

Outside of the nurses and the doctor that delivered the baby I was alone.

My mother wasn't there to talk me through the pain. she wasn't there to reassure me that everything was going to be okay.

I gave birth to a beautiful 7 lb 9 oz baby boy that was 21 and 1/2 inches Long.

I dealt with the pain and pushed him out naturally.

When my mother finally made it to the hospital the next day, she walked into my room and looked at my baby.

I can't even remember what she said to me. I just remember her turning around and walking away. She didn't bring any gifts for the baby.

There were no congratulations, you did well. No balloons or flowers with it's a boy on it.

I can understand how she felt about me being pregnant as a teenager, however, it was still her grandson and I was still her daughter.

Once I got home with the baby things got even harder.

Now I had a baby I had to provide for.

R did what he could to help me to make sure the baby had what he needed in the beginning.

Thank God for Sister, sister had so much stuff from her baby leftover that she shared with me. And when I say R helped in the beginning, that's because after the baby was born the ex-girlfriend or whatever started the drama.

Campaigning.

R's life also went from one extreme to the next, he was in an altercation and was locked up.

Once R got out of the county jail he enlisted into the military. Something he had planned before going to jail.

6 months after my son was born he left.

The first six to eight weeks were the worst, basic training.

He would write to me every week and I received weekly phone calls. He sent me one money order for $19.89.

That was all the money he had at that point he hadn't got his first check from the military.

And then the letters stop coming.

Everything was going fine between him and me and I couldn't understand what was going on.

I would write to him and he wouldn't respond.

And then the day came when he was home to visit. I had heard that he was coming home from his sister Shonda.

R and Shonda were very close. She and I became close after he left to go into the army.

When R came home he came to see me and his son Little R, Yes I named him after his father. He was happy.

We were happy for the moment.

I remember sitting in his room talking to him about the military and he was unpacking his clothes.

R had a bigfoot so his shoes were a big thing to him.

And he had just bought a pair of Stacy Adams that was the popular shoe at that time.

This fool picked our son up and placed him in the shoe box, that's how big his foot was. He had found a pair of Stacy Adams that no one in the city would have so he had to show me those.

After the visit with R, I returned home.

My mother was waiting for me with a full speech.

The First thing she said to me was, Don't sleep with him! I didn't understand where that came from. But those were her words. R was only home for 2 weeks and I'm pretty sure he made his rounds when he was home.

When he came to the house she let him stay all night.

He slept in my room with me and I kept the door open. Wide-open so she could see clearly through the room. I never slept with him in my mother's house. When the two weeks were over it was time for him to leave.

After he left we kept in touch through letters and phone calls and then everything just stopped. That was the beginning of the End.

CHAPTER 21

No Money More problems

I'm at home living with my mother and I have a baby. My sister has a son that is a year older than my son, and then my mother has my brother that's a year older than my nephew.

The three of us and three babies.

Every day it was like walking on eggshells.

Every day it was an argument and sometimes physical.

Sister had a bad habit of getting up in the middle of the night and sneaking out of the house leaving the baby.

I would hear him crying and get up and get him. Sometimes she would be gone for two days. And it was something that she did often. My sister and my mother would fight all the time about that.

The only thing my mother couldn't say is that my sister didn't have what she needed for the baby.

She could fuss about how she got it, but he was never without.

And when it came to my son, I knew my mother was getting a check for my son as well as a check for my sister.

Every first of the month it would be something.

If she gave us anything it would be $20.00 if we got that.

What can you do with $20.00 for a baby?. Maybe buy a Big bag of Pampers at that time. There were times I had to go to my grandmother for money for the baby.

We had our good days and we had our bad days. When my mother wasn't dealing with me and my sister she had her relationship to deal with.

The relationship with my brother's father.

I guess this is where they had a bump in the road. By this time the other woman had put pressure on him to marry her, now he's a married man.

It didn't stop him from seeing my mother.

He would visit when she allowed him to.

The last Thanksgiving that I spent in my mother's house, was the first time that I cooked a full Thanksgiving meal.

The day before Thanksgiving, that evening, my mother was preparing her Thanksgiving meal, prepping all the food.

I remember she had all the eyes on the stove burning with pots on them, something cooking in every pot.

Everything she was cooking was on the table, the turkey was on the table.

As my mother was cooking there was a knock at the door.

It was the HPD, they had a warrant for my mother's arrest.

An assault warrant for something my mother didn't do.

My mother explained to the police that she was cooking our Thanksgiving dinner and that there was no one home with us.

It didn't matter because they took her to jail anyway.

I was old enough to be responsible for my sisters, brother, and nephew.

The police took my mother to jail and because it was a holiday weekend she would be in jail for the whole weekend until Monday.

So now I'm left standing in the kitchen looking at my mother's food.

I was the one that was always in the kitchen that helped cook so I could remember how she prepared some of the dishes.

The one thing about that night that bothers me the most is the fact that when they arrested my mother and took her to jail, the witch was standing across the street watching.

And it was dark outside.

You always see evil in the darkness.

I was able to prepare the food to the best of my ability.

After my mother was released from jail she did her best to move on past that situation.

It didn't change what we were going through in the house.

Once again we're arguing about money. After some time R reached out to me through his sister.

He wanted to know why I wasn't responding to his letters, he also said that he had sent me a few money orders.

So I asked my mother about the mail and she said I didn't get any mail.

Now I'm upset because I had just talked with R.

Then I asked her about the money from the welfare that started a whole war!.

I went to talk to my Grandmother about the money situation with my Mother. I even spoke with my aunt about the matter and the results were the same.

My Grandmother told me I was old enough to get a check for myself and to go up and talk to the caseworker.

She even told me that I was old enough to get it for my sister and her baby too.

I did just that.

I went and talked to the caseworker about the check.

I had a relationship with the caseworker already from years prior.

So now I'm coming to the very lady that helped me get my mother's assistance, for help to get assistance for myself and my sister.

I did this without my mother's knowledge not understanding the aftermath!

The change didn't come automatically, it took a little time.

However, in the process, other things were happening. mother and sister began to physically fight.

It seemed like if it wasn't me it was my sister.

Now let me say this, my mother always told us that she loved us!.

Even if it was after she had beat the hell out of one of us.

I never questioned my mother's love for me, I just didn't think she liked me sometimes.

I would do everything I could to stay away from my mother's house with my baby, and that's only when she would let me go.

My older sister had got an apartment in the projects so I would try and visit her as much as I could.

I was coming home with my baby from my sister's apartment down the street one afternoon.

As I got closer to the house I could hear someone screaming or fussing with someone.

I made it to my house and it was my mother and my sister.

My mother and sister were fighting in the yard.

When I came across the street I heard my sister screaming, and when I looked at her, I noticed that she was bleeding between her legs, and my mother was hitting her.

After I broke them up my sister had to go to the hospital.

After my sister returned home from the hospital, she and I started talking about moving out.

We didn't know how but we knew we wanted to move.

Until then we had to abide by her rules in her house. I realized by having a baby 2 weeks before I turned 18 that what little freedom I had was gone.

I shouldn't say that my freedom was gone but now I had a baby that had to go with me. And really what was the difference? I was always dragging one of my siblings behind me anyway.

Most of the time I stayed at home with my baby and I would babysit for my sister.

My brother would be at home too with my mother so I would be at home spending time with the babies. and being at home I would always see a lot of things that would happen in the complex just looking out of the window.

CHAPTER 22

My casa is your casa.

Cousin #1, was the nephew of the man that said he wasn't my father.

When I was about 15 I was introduced to his mother and that's how I met my cousins #1 and #2. From that point on we developed the relationship, we knew we were cousins.

It didn't matter what that man said.
My cousin came to visit me a couple of times after that.

He also had a friend he played basketball with that lived in the projects across the street from me.

So when he would go over there to visit he would come across the street to visit me.

One day my cousin came to see me and on this particular visit, he and his mother had gotten into it and she put him out.

After we talked about it, I asked my mother if he could stay with us.

My mother said yes and he moved in.
#1 was gone a lot, he played basketball all the time and he also had a girlfriend or two.

That's how I met Nugget.
Nugget was from Middletown, Franklin Ohio.
And she would come to Hamilton to see cousin #1
She worked as a manager at Pizza hut and was always working. She had a car and her own money.
And she didn't mind sharing.

When she had free time she would come and see cousin#1 and we had time to spend together also.
Nugget was a really fun person to hang around.
She was Tall and Beautiful!
With a beautiful smile.
Nugget came from a good family.

Over time she and I developed a friendship. we had gotten close to the point that I would take my son and spend the night at our mother's house.

Her family was always so nice to me they made me feel welcome.
I would spend the night at her family's home in Franklin.
They lived in the subdivision, one of the first subdivisions built out in Franklin. There were only three houses on the street.

I was close to home however it seemed far away.
That was my getaway when I could get away.
The last time I visited, Nugget's mother was getting her hair done. and by accident, she picked up the wrong cup and sipped it. The cup contained the chemicals for her hair.

She had to go to the hospital.
She was already a soft-spoken woman.

I'm pretty sure it did some damage to her throat. Outside of that all of my experiences were fun when I stayed at the Nugget family's house.

For a while, things seem to be going well. Since my cousin was around my Mother wasn't as strict.
She was going through changes with the Father of my brother and she also started reading her Bible more.

Learning about Jehovah.

Every chance she got to share Jehovah's word she shared. Even with my cousin.
Living in my mother's house for the next several months was never a dull moment.

CHAPTER 23

Love and War

Every day was a new experience.
And more than likely something was going to happen.

Be it good or bad, it was always something.

When the days were good they were really good. And when the days were bad they were really bad.

MTV was the thing at the time.
To be able to watch music videos was something new.
Michael Jackson Thriller came out that year and my little brother was scared of the video.
Every time the video came on he would just run away from the TV.

The Temptations, Treat her Like a Lady was in rotation Every 30 minutes.

The video played so much that my Nephew K.C., knew the words to the song.

I just happened to hear him singing one day.
His mother had just bathed him and dressed him with his hair slicked down with baby magic and Vaseline.

He was sitting at the bottom of the steps. The steps in the projects were made of steel, so he's kicking his feet on the back of the stairs to the beat and rubbing his hands together singing, Treat her Like a Lady!

Sitting there with that little pie face of his, all shined up and smelling good in his little outfit waiting for his mother to take him outside.
I said from that point that he was going to be a lady's man.
That was a good day.

When I say bad days, sometimes it depends on who was on the other side of the door when you answered it.

My mother had a thing about answering the door.

If she was asleep, do not answer the door and wake her up!

And she constantly reminded my little sisters about not answering the door.

When we lived on Walnut it was the first of the month. Little Sister was coming in from school and a man walked into the house behind her and stole the mail.

At that time my mother was getting a check and food stamps and they delivered the benefits in the mail.

One afternoon I was at home babysitting. Sister was gone and so was my Mother.

My cousin had gone to play basketball or visit a friend I can't remember.

So it's me and the babies, little sister and baby sister.

It's a knock at the door and as usual, Little sister runs to the door. And I say don't answer that door!.

So I went to the door and answered it and it was my cousin "E".

"E" is my cousin and he is the nephew of the man that is said to be my father.

He was 27 and married with two children.

He was looking for our cousin.

He wanted to return his keys because he had borrowed his car.

I stood in the doorway talking to him for a few minutes.

The thing about my relationship with my cousin "E" was, from the first time we met each other he was the one that let me know we were related.

And he always looked out for me as if he was always in my life.

If he was to see me on the block, he would give me a few dollars and send me away from the block.

Made sure I was okay and no one was bothering me.

I felt protected when I was around him.

I never felt afraid.

After He and I talked, he gave me the keys and smiled at me, then he walked away.

I stood there staring at him as he walked away.

I followed him through the house looking through the windows and ended up at the back door.

I watched him until I couldn't see him anymore.

As he was walking past the cage, I noticed something strange.

He was wearing a woman's coat.

I didn't pay any attention at the time.

I just thought it was strange.

And I went on about my day.

A few days later I was on my way out the front door and the police and the detectives were in the parking lot surrounding my cousin's car.

The detectives had everything pulled out of the car.
The floor mats everything he had in the car was out on the trunk or the ground.

And then they towed the car away.
It was all over the news and the newspaper.

Murder on the west side.
And my cousin "E" was charged with Murder.
He was charged for the death of his wife's best friend.

Looking back on it, trying to find some understanding of such a bizarre situation took me on a journey to find an understanding for myself.

When something this Traumatic happens in the city, by the time the Hood hears it the story has been changed a million times.

However Sitting in that courtroom looking at the evidence, listening to the prosecutor and the defense go back and forth.

The character witnesses testimony.
And then to listen to the accused testify and tell his side of the story.

I sat there with so many thoughts running through my head.

I remember my heart beating real fast.
The anxiety was setting in, and at that time I didn't understand what that was.
I just know that each day that I went to the courthouse and sat through that trial, it began to make me sick.
I would have this pain in my stomach that wouldn't go away.
From each word and the lies that came out of the prosecutor's mouth to every piece of evidence, I was consumed by it all.
The testimony from the Family of the victim was heartbreaking and full of grief.

From the testimony of my cousin, I witnessed a man that stood accountable for his actions.
And in all reality, he had no choice.
And it takes a man to admit his faults.

From every detail, in his truth, he left no details out.
He stood accountable for his actions in the court of law.

God Is The Real Judge.
His wife, the mother of his children's testimony, left me confused and thinking.

The guilty verdict that was to be expected!.

However, the sentence of 45 to life at 27 years old, left me wondering if he had never been with that white woman would this have happened?.

With the all-white jury, there was no way he was going to get a fair trial, not in this city.

CHAPTER 24

I Mean No Disrespect

After my cousin's murder trial, I tried to get back to normal if there was a normal.

It was a good thing that my sister moved down the street, I was able to go visit with her and talk and just get away from everything.

I was getting away from everything but it was plenty to get into, and that I did.
I started spending more time at my sister's house.
It was her first apartment and she made the rules in her house.
I could go there and just be myself and have a good time. We always had a good time.
We had so much of a good time that one night we double-dated, with the father of her son and his best friend.

I guess we called ourselves being grown. We called ourselves having drinks and I wasn't even drinking at the time.

I tried it that night and the next thing I know I ended up in the shower with the friend having sex.
That's just one of the nights we called ourselves having fun. Trust me it was many more.
Many more days of what I thought was fun.

Doing what I wanted to do, thinking I was grown. I didn't have a boyfriend, however, I knew a lot of Young men my age.
And during that period in time, this is when I became promiscuous.

I'm pretty sure I'm not the only one that had a promiscuous stage in their lives, at least those of us that are willing to admit it.
And for those that didn't experience it, Life goes on.

Back at home, I found myself not wanting to be there. I began to think about getting an apartment.
And I knew at that point that I had a baby and that I could get a check and move out of my

mother's house. for a few weeks, everything in the house would be okay and then something would happen.

I would spend as much time as I could away from the house. Nugget would pick me up and we would spend time at her house in Franklin or just ride around in her car.

Taking long rides in the car listening to music and looking at people.
It's nothing like stopping at a red light when your song is on the radio.
She would put the car in park, and get out and start dancing in the middle of traffic.
We did that!.
Our conversations would last most of the night when I stayed over.

We would have long conversations about everything. me being a young mother and I was breastfeeding at the time.
And that's something girls my age weren't breastfeeding.

She was my cousin's girlfriend and that's how I met her.
She ended up being a really good friend to me.
She was also the one I would confide in when I found out that I was pregnant again.

That night in the shower caught up with me.
Having a good time, or so I thought.
She was the first person I told.

I knew my mother was going to have a fit!.
I didn't want to have another baby.
I didn't even know I was pregnant.
Pregnant with a child that I didn't need.

I can't even remember how I came up with the plan to get an abortion. And to get the abortion without my Mother knowing I was even pregnant.
It wasn't about talking to the person that I was pregnant by, I was not having a baby and it was my choice. So once I got everything taken care of as far as the appointment and the money to pay for the procedure.
The morning of, I was getting into the car with Nugget, to go and have the abortion.

As I was about to get in the car and leave my mother came to the back door and said to me, I know you're not about to go down there and kill my granddaughter.

She wasn't asking a question, she was making a statement!.

I stood there stuck.
I didn't know what to say. I don't know how she found out, I never told her I was pregnant.

Lady J.

So now she knows I'm pregnant and she also knows I want to have an abortion.

I think it was the look that she gave me and the tone of her voice that made me change my mind. And I knew I had to get out of that house, hell I was afraid to go in the house.

After a few minutes of talking with Nugget, I told her that I would call her later and I went into the house.
When I went into the house my mother didn't say anything to me.
She didn't mention it for a few days.
And then the day the mail came.
The mail came and my mother found out that the welfare was going to cut off her money.

When I say all hell broke loose, All Hell Broke Loose!.
At the same time, my cousin was moving out.
He was moving into an apartment or with someone.

The shit didn't hit the fan until after he left.

There were a few arguments when he was around and he would try to keep the peace in the house while he was there.

Now let me say this, My mother didn't put me out.

I knew sooner or later I was going to have to leave. It was her house and no matter what I did it was always something wrong.

The physical abuse had gotten to the point that it was going to be me or her!.
And the thing was, she was my mother and I couldn't disrespect her by putting my hands on her to fight her.
I witnessed her and my sister fight.
I just couldn't do it.
The verbal abuse I learned to deal with I could almost block it out. Her words would cut Like a knife.
What else could she say to me, that she hadn't already said.
My mother let me know that I wasn't shit more than a few times.

When Everything came to a head.
Her words got louder because she was in my face and she slapped me.

She then put her hands around my neck and choked me up off of my feet.
At that point, I snapped!.

I grabbed her by the wrist and took her hands off of my neck and I held them.

I backed her up and I said to her," You Will Not Hit Me Again!" I did not hit my mother or even exchange words with her.

What I did was, got my baby and my things and I left her house.

I left my mother's house with a baby on my hip, a baby in my stomach, and a bag of clothes in my hand. I Never Looked Back!
The Cycle.

CHAPTER 25

Where Do I Go From Here

When I left my Mother's house I didn't have a plan and didn't know where I was going.

The only thing that mattered was that I was leaving.
Leaving what I consider hell.

The first place I went was to my Grandmother's house.

I think my Grandmother knew this day would come.

When I made it to my grandmother's house she was sitting on the porch.

I walked up on the porch and I was crying. She asked me what was wrong. I told her that I just got into it with mom and I left.

So as we're talking, a few minutes later my Mother walks up. she didn't just walk up she walked up yelling and screaming, and she tried to hit me.

I ran and stood behind my grandmother.
My grandmother said to her, You're are not going to hit her again!

That only made my mother go off, she was furious! she started yelling and screaming at my Grandmother.

She was saying all kinds of things. She told my Grandmother that she was picking sides and that she believed anything that I told her.
And whatever I was saying was a lie. Mom was so upset that she snatched the TV antenna wire off the side of the house.

At that time the antennas were on top of the house.
My Grandmother wasn't afraid of her and she let her know that was her house and to go away from there with all that messing up her words.

My Grandmother was a peaceful and calm woman. and for the most part that's how she tried to deal with everything as far as I could see, Peacefully.

As my Mother turned to walk away her last words to my Grandmother on that day were, "YOU DEAD TO ME!.

My Grandmother was looking at my mother shaking her head side to side. and then she turned to me as she was opening the screen door for me to go into the house and said, "Something is wrong with her".

Once things calmed down and I explained everything to my grandmother, I can say that she was disappointed in my mother.

However, she was also disappointed in me.

Here I am pregnant again and I'm not even 20 years old yet. I stayed with my Grandmother on and off for about 6 months. With my grandmother, I had a little more freedom.
She would give me time by keeping my son for a few hours.
And most of the time I didn't make it very far because my son was a crybaby.

All he did was cry, cry, cry. there would be times I would try to leave and I would only make it to the corner and my Grandmother would be calling me back.

He was what they call spoiled.
I breastfed him and I held him a lot.
Up until the point that I started showing, I was able to do normal things. I hung out with my girlfriends.

I even hung out with a few guys. No one knew I was pregnant. Then I moved in with my Aunt and her husband, my mother's baby sister.

I stayed with them for a little while and then it was time to get my first apartment.
I found a little one-bedroom house off of an alley.
The alley behind my aunt's house. It was a three-room shed. I had a very small kitchen, a very small living room, a very small bedroom and they made a bathroom next to the small bedroom.

I moved in with very little. My Aunt and her husband helped me a lot, they gave me a living room set and a refrigerator to start.

It would be just me and my babies so I didn't need much.
I finally have my place.

A place where my friends could come and visit, and I made the rules.

I could come and go as I please.

Lady J.

Nugget would come and visit often.

On her days off or when she got off from work early. we would go riding around in her car, to get ice cream or something to eat.

She came by so much that I gave her a key.

At this time we didn't have cell phones and I didn't have a house phone. I would have to go to my aunt's or my grandmother's to use the phone.
Or walk down the street a block and use the payphone. So I gave Nugget a key just in case she came to Hamilton and I wasn't home.
By the time I got settled into my apartment, my cousin moved in with me.

Wherever he had moved to was temporary.

And because he was my cousin I wouldn't see him out in the streets. or maybe it was the fact that I wanted a relationship with my father so bad that I would have done anything to get closer to him, My Father.

And I was also doing what I felt was right by my family.
So now I'm trying to be grown and on my own, and my cousin is living with me.

From the time I left my mother's house until the time the baby came a lot of things had occurred. and at that point, I hadn't even told the father that I was pregnant. I had my reasons.

CHAPTER 26

June 25, 1985

My baby was born.

A Beautiful little Chocolate girl.

By the time I gave birth to my daughter, I had a few guy friends that I was dealing with on and off. so it was a big question of who the baby's father was as far as the other people were concerned.

I had my reasons for not saying who the father was. And other people's assumptions gave way to a lie that I helped grow.

Having my place wasn't easy and being a mother was even harder.
It was all on me.
The last time I had any communication with R was when he returned from basic training and I found out that my mother was keeping the mail from me.

Now I have another child without a father.

My Mother and my Grandmother let me know that this was something that I was going to have to do on my own because of the choices that I made.

CHAPTER 27

Somebody Got To Go

Blood doesn't make us family.
My cousin and I. we were too much alike.

So much alike that we clashed when it came to certain things.
And I have to be perfectly honest as I write this piece.
In the beginning, things were okay.

I even felt protected with him being in the house with me, because the house was in the alley.

Like I said in the beginning everything was okay, we had a lot of fun.

When he wasn't out playing basketball or out doing whatever he was doing we would be at the house.
Laughing and talking all night. One thing my cousin could do was crack a joke.

Over time we began to bump heads over moral issues, and it was his way or no way.

My cousin was selfish and he only thought about himself!. He did what he wanted to do when he wanted to do it.

When I say he took My Casa is your Casa to another level.
He even allowed his partner to bring a random chick to my house when I wasn't there.
His partner was dating Nugget's sister at the time.
And if my memory serves me correctly, she being Nuggets sister, walked in on him and another girl.
Him being my cousin's partner/best friend at the time.

My cousin ate what he wanted to eat when he wanted to eat it.
It didn't matter if it was snacks for the kids.

His IDGAF personality took over my house without even contributing a dollar.

For me I thought I was looking out for my cousin, I was about to find out what the family will do to you and why his mother put him out.

It all started with the door key that I had given Nugget months before.

On this particular day, she came to town and by chance, I was not at home.

The only time she used the key was the day that my cousin was in the house with another female.

One of the little twins that lived down the street from my Grandmother's house.

Keep in mind she had the key to my house before my cousin moved in. So it wasn't like I gave her the key to keep an eye on him or anything like that.

Before all that was ever explained, The Shit hit the fan!.
I came home from being out.

As I reached the corner of the street that I lived on, Nuggets cousin was standing on the corner holding her shoes in her hand.

And she says to me, If I didn't have these shoes on I would have helped.

I didn't know what she was talking about so I walked up the street to my house.
As I reached the alley, Nuggets sister was lying in the alley crying.
I could hear Nugget screaming and yelling and I could also hear my cousin.

As I walked into the house my cousin was on top of her choking her and hitting her.

I walked up behind him to try and pull him off of her.
When he turned around and looked at me, he let her go and grabbed me by the neck.

The look on his face when he turned around it was almost like seeing the devil.

I don't know what the devil looks like, but I'm pretty sure that was close to it, in a physical form.
He's choking me, he's hitting me and he slammed down on the floor.

As I'm hitting him and digging my fingernails into him and hitting him trying to get him off of Me.

I'm calling his name and I'm trying to get him to snap back in, he had snapped out!.

The anger and the rage that came out of him, I could not believe what I was experiencing.

I had never seen anyone my age do that at this point. Beat a girl up.

I hadn't experienced that since I was a little girl and the man across the park would beat up his wife.

Or the time I saw a black man that I knew from the neighborhood beating up a white prostitute.

So now I'm in the house with it and I'm being beat on too.

Once he let me go he was yelling at me and calling me all kinds of Bitches, saying that I wasn't shit saying, I set him up and I gave her the key on purpose.

And that was not the truth!. And that was the day he had to leave my house.

From that day to this day, I will never have an understanding of how he could hurt me when I was looking out for him. Even more, I couldn't understand how he could do Nugget the way he did.
How he could just beat her like that.

She was such a good girl and she was good to him.
She was there whenever he called her and she also did anything he asked. She loved him.

She loved him when he had no respect for her.
Not soon after I put him out of my house, my relationship with Nugget would slowly come to an end.

At the time I didn't understand. Looking at it now I guess it was for the best.

She deserves better and I didn't want to be the reason that he beat her up.
It was for the best.
Now it's just me and the kids, but it wasn't that way for long.

CHAPTER 28

Dr. Jekyll And Mr. Hyde

Mr. Cincinnati was someone that I had met one day while I was taking a walk with my kids. He was riding his motorcycle and he was from out of town.

He pulled up alongside me as I was walking. He stopped me and we talked for a little while.

We exchanged numbers but I didn't pay him any attention. He could only call me at my grandmother's house and I didn't live there, so by chance if I was there we would talk or he would leave a message for me to call him.

Once I allowed him into my space things began to move quickly.

At this time in my life, I had two children and I hadn't had a boyfriend yet, this would be my first relationship.

All of the things that I wanted, or at least I thought I wanted in a boyfriend he was.

In the beginning.

He accepted my children.

When I say this man would give me gifts just because.

He worked downtown Cincinnati at the Hyatt regency and every week when he got paid, I got an allowance.

I couldn't even get money from my mother so to have him, my boyfriend gives me money was a big thing.

He would take me out to eat, me and the kids. And he would look out for my kids as well. When he bought something for me he bought something for them.

The way he presented himself to my children I never experienced that, not even with their father.

Everything that occurred happened within a year. Now I met him in my city and he had been coming up here for some time. So he had a couple of guy friends that he knew before he met me, that knew of me. so I really can't say how long he had been watching me. I just know everything moved fast.

On our first Christmas together he bought the kids everything and he gifted me with gold jewelry.

My Grandmother used to say, sometimes you have to be careful of people bearing gifts.
In this relationship, I found out what she was talking about.

The first 6 months of the relationship were fine. I was learning things I didn't know, like I said in the beginning we were moving fast.

And he was learning about me as well.

At that time I didn't drink or smoke or do any drugs. The last time I called myself being grown and drinking I got pregnant with my daughter.

On the other hand, he liked to drink. I didn't have a problem with that.
And from what I understand he came from a family that likes to drink.

Or should I say they like to have a good time or maybe it was always something to drink around? I don't know what it was.

And with that drinking came learned behavior.
The first time I saw him heavily intoxicated I experienced the other side of him.

The alcohol made him act like a different person and I soon found myself in the same situation that my friend was in.

I'm in a relationship with an abusive man, Dr. Jekyll Mr. Hyde.

When he wasn't drinking he was the nicest man you would ever want to meet, and when he was drinking you never knew what was going to happen.

The abuse started slowly.
It started verbally.

Our problems always started behind a rumor. Like I said he had friends in my city before he met me.

It would be times that he would go and have a few beers with the fellas after playing basketball and he would come home tripping.
If it wasn't one thing it was another. Someone would tell him something about me or it would be a female that was trying to talk to him, would tell him shit just to fuck.

Someone always had a story about me to tell him. and when he came home I would have to defend myself against the Bullshit.

Like I said it started small. The verbal abuse then turned into a push.

The push turned into a slap and the slap eventually turned into a beating.
When all this was going on I couldn't understand why.

What was I doing wrong?
When he was at work I was at home taking care of the kids.
I spent all of my time with him. I would go to his mother's house, me and the kids, and stay the weekend.
I was always with him.
I couldn't do anything. So I made sure he knew where I was and what I was doing at all times.
That only stopped the beating for so long.

Then I realized this was just the person that I was with. I started spending more time at his mother's house, I thought that would change things. I thought with me being there at his mother's house he would see that I wasn't doing the things that people were saying I was doing.
That was a quick fix; it only lasted so long. After a while, I knew that I had to get away from him.

So I began to try and distance myself from him. Most of the time it was unsuccessful because he would always come back when I would make him leave. for some and I would let him stay.

I was so confused about the whole situation I had never dealt with anything like that before.

One of the times, because there were many, that I broke up with him I decided to see someone else.
And by this time I learned that each time we broke up, he would go back to Cincinnati and be with his ex-girlfriend and that he had a baby on the way with another girl.

At that point, I had enough so I was trying to get on with my life.
I'll never forget it, it was on the weekend and I hooked up with one of my friends.
He owned a house on the Westside of Hamilton.

I had arranged for my children to stay overnight with an older lady by the name of
Miss Clara Barnett.

Miss Barnett would babysit and help me with the kids whenever I needed her and she was very good at caring for children.
She would feed them and wash their clothes out by hand.
I don't know anyone to this day that could hand wash clothes the way Miss Barnett would wash them.

She would rinse them with that Downy and hang the clothes on the clothesline. on a beautiful sunny day when you would walk by there, you would smell the scent of her clean clothes blowing in the wind.
Well back to the story...
Me and Mr. Cincinnati were broken up and I decided to link up with a friend.

Lady J.

I was gone all night and I had to pick the kids up the next day by noon. as my friend was about to drop me off at my house he circled the block a couple of times.

We had spent most of the night talking about life and my problems so he was making sure the scene was safe to let me out.

As he pulled up to the corner of Hanover and Lane Street, I lived on Hanover Street. My house was in the alley, I happened to see Mr. Cincinnati's car so my friend continued to drive away from the house.

He hit a few corners and then he drove in the direction of the Westside.

I can't say that Mr. Cincinnati was sitting there waiting, watching, and saw me or if someone told him.

All I know is that the chase was on!.

From the Eastside to the south side to the west side, Mr. Cincinnati was driving behind my friend's car and he was driving fast.

He was driving so fast that at one point he caught up to the car and pulled on the side and looked me right in my face.

We made eye contact and at that point, I knew he was heated!.

After a couple of minutes of the drag race, I told my friend to drop me off in the projects at the babysitter.

My friend was hesitant at first. He was like no, let me pull over I'm going to beat this "Nigga's" ass! And he had his gun in the car.

I told him no, just take me to the babysitter and drop me off.

Mr. Cincinnati followed us to the projects. My friend kept asking me if I wanted him to walk me to the door, did I need him to wait and take us home?. I told him no to go on, I'll be okay.

My Mother lived two rolls over from the babysitter's house so I thought maybe things would be okay.

By the time I had gotten out of my friend's car and made it halfway to the babysitter's door Mr. Cincinnati had run up on me.

He first asked me where I've been and who I was with?. I told him to go on and leave me alone and that we weren't together.

This only made him even angrier!.
He kept saying, "you got to go home".

Before I knew it this man had slapped me, snatched me up by my shirt, and Dropped kicked me. And he wasn't finished there; he had a few choice words for me.

When he was done calling me everything except the child of God, he spits in my face as I was laying on the ground holding my stomach.

He's standing over me and he tells me to go in the house and get the kids. I don't know if Miss Barnett saw it, I tried to act as nothing was wrong. I got the kids and I paid her and we went home.

And when I say we, I mean myself, my children, and Mr. Cincinnati.

The crazy thing about being in an abusive relationship is, the same person that you love that makes you feel so good can be the very person to hurt you and make you feel so bad.

Confused, I was so confused and afraid to talk to anyone about it. I mean I had just witnessed my cousin beating on his girlfriend and I couldn't even understand what that was all about, so now I'm dealing with it myself.

Confused, Hell that's an understatement. We would be okay for a couple of weeks and then boom, something would happen and we would fight. Let me correct myself, he would want to fight.

He would try and provoke me to argue and that would sometimes lead up to a fight, way into the wee hours of the morning.

And after calling me every Whore and Bitch that he could think of, he would Cry And Apologize for everything he had just done and said to me.

He would Cry to the point that I cried with him, afterward we would have sex.

The kind of sex that I now know to be toxic!.
I guess it's what's called, make-up sex.

The kind of sex that is filled with passion, confusion, and lots of emotion.
A relationship can only last so long this way.

And then it happened.
Everything was okay Until he went out with his friends from Cincinnati one night and I stayed at the house with his mother.
He came home about 2:00-2:30 in the morning and he woke me up!
He was upset.
He had me wake the kids up and he wanted to come back to Hamilton.

The way he came in and woke me up I knew something was wrong and he had been drinking. I could smell the alcohol.

The drive from his mother's house in Cincinnati to Hamilton was about 40 minutes.
He was driving so fast it seemed like we made it home in 15 minutes or less.
Once we made it into the house he started going off on me.

77

He was saying things like I was a Whore and that he knew I was Fucking around on him the whole time. he said he knew about all the men I had been with, and that I was making him look like a fool.

We argued back and forth for about an hour. Somewhere around 4 am, he began to beat me.

After the beating he made me have sex with him.

He made me have sex with him when I didn't want to. In his mind, he was proving that he was man enough for me.

And the only reason that I say that is because he kept asking me, he kept asking me if he was man enough for me.

And the whole time that he's asking me if he's man enough he's violating my body.

He did everything he wanted to do to me. It was after 7:30 the next morning when he stopped, the sun was up and the birds were chirping.

I will never forget the way he hit me in my mouth and then kissed the blood from my swollen lips.

And the most confusing part of it all was, how he would cry and break down apologizing.

I was so confused because I believed him. I even cried with him when he was apologizing.

That's confusing and twisted.

I didn't know what to expect. I didn't know what to do. I just knew something wasn't right. something started clicking in my head. After that night he chilled out for a while and he was back to normal.

It seemed like he apologized forever.

After the fact, That's was only after the next morning when he had to look at my swollen face from him hitting me.

He promised that he would never do it again. I came to learn that when that happened, I had at least three more ass whoopings coming.

I got to the point where I hated being around him and I didn't know how to get him away from me.

When I tried to talk about the abuse and the relationship no one believed me.

Everyone thought he was such a good guy. I could say that at that time, it was a price I was paying for everything that he gave me. and The crazy thing about that was, I never asked him for anything!. It was like, being in that little house was just driving me crazy. Maybe it was just being in the house with him and I didn't know how to get away from him.

Soon the house wouldn't be a problem.

CHAPTER 29

Up In Smoke

Over the next couple of months, Mr. Cincinnati was doing everything he could to prove to me that he had changed.

On this particular payday, Mr. Cincinnati made plans to take me and the kids shopping and out to eat.

We planned to go to Cincinnati for the day and spend the night at his mother's.

Once we made it to his mother's house everything was fine. Later that evening I got a phone call at his mother's house from the Hamilton Police dispatcher.

Once I answered the call the dispatcher was asking me, are your children with you? And she also had my grandmother on the line.

My Grandmother said my name and asked me if the kids were with me. I told her yes, why what's going on?.

The dispatcher then took over the phone call and said that I needed to come to Hamilton because my house was on fire and they thought the kids were in the house. so we leave Cincinnati and head to Hamilton.

Before we even made it to the City of Fairfield we're on Hamilton avenue and I could see the SMOKE, the black smoke in the sky from my house in Hamilton burning.

When I finally got to the house I could not believe my eyes.

My first place, my little home, was burning. It was so bad that after a while they let the house burn.

I lost everything! The few things I had acquired for my place.

When we went shopping, we stopped by the house and dropped the items off before we left. the new clothes we had just bought.

When I say everything burned, the only thing left was a charred coffee table and two end tables.

I went through the drawers of the end table where I kept my important papers.

Everything was burned except for my children's birth certificates and a 10x13 family portrait I had made of the kids and me.

I took that as a sign from God. I could have lost my children or my own life in that fire.

So for that, I was thankful.

The Red Cross came in and helped with a place to stay for a few nights. and helped me with the things that I would need to start all over.

We also found another apartment on the same street. Hanover Street. 345 Hanover, It was a two-bedroom.

It was a somewhat decent apartment better than the shed I was living in.

There was only 1 door, raised half an inch from the floor so I would have to keep a towel up to the door to keep the mice and anything else from coming under the door.

I didn't have this problem at the new place.

I had two doors and two screen doors.
Starting over, moving gives you a good feeling.
A good feeling that didn't last long.

Once we moved in together and he started helping with the bills things got worse.

He became very controlling. We began to argue a lot and being in the house with him was unbearable at times.

Being that he was the man of the house now, he was setting the rules for everything.

He began to drink more.

It seemed as if once a week he was putting his hands on me in some way.
He had to prove his point that he was the man.
He felt as if he had a point to prove to the men in the city that he thought I was with.

I can say it began to be a love-hate relationship.
Some days I wanted to be there, other days I didn't.
In the process, my nerves started getting bad. And my hair started falling out.

It was falling out so bad that I had to do something to it and just by chance on a visit to Mr. Cincinnati's Mother's house, we drove by a beauty shop on California avenue by the name of Hairpin.

We stopped and the owner of the shop made a walk-in appointment for me.

This would be the first and one of the three times that I paid to have a hair weaved in my life.

I was the first one in my city to wear one. That I knew of.

Can you imagine the backlash that I received from it?
Everyone was talking about me and my fake hair.
It bothered them more than it bothered me.

I even noticed a change in Mr. Cincinnati.
He began to be insecure.

Every day was something different.
So in my head, I'm trying to figure out what to do and how to get away from him, me, and my children.
That was kind of hard to do with both of them being so little.

The abuse began to be routine.
And I began to recognize the signs.
It would be the look in his eyes or the tone of his voice.
I could tell when he was about to go there with me.
So I started watching and I was very careful not to upset him.
In the back of my mind, I knew one day this was going to be over and I was going to get away from him.

CHAPTER 30

The Beginning Of The End

My sister Tracy's house was my only place of refuge.
I could go visit my sister and Mr. Cincinnati didn't have a problem with it.
For some reason, he felt secure with my sister, not understanding she was My sister.
She was the one I could talk to about the problems in my relationship or life.

She knew very little about what was going on. I kept most of the abuse to myself.

We could always joke about it.

We would always say how we would fuck up each other's boyfriends if we had to.

We not only talked about it, but we also did it!.
Case and point, the father of her sons, was good for starting some shit.

I can say for certain we jumped his ass at least once!.
So she was always on standby just in case.
My sister's keeper.

And then the day came that I needed her.

I didn't know that night would be the night that I would be freed from that relationship.

It all started when Mr. Cincinnati came home from work and he wanted to go out for a little while with the guys and have a few beers.
I didn't have a problem with that.
I stayed at the house while he went out and he came home after it got dark.
Once he came into the house, he said he wanted to go up the street for a little while.

Up the street meant he wanted to go on the square, where the nigga's hung out at.

That very moment, something in my head told me to tell him to take me to my sister's while he went out.

He gladly did because he didn't want me to be upset about the fact that he asked to go back out after he had just come into the house.

I had a feeling that something bad was going to happen that night, he was just too giddy about going up the street.

He dropped me and the kids off at my sister's house.

A week before he had jumped on me. the next morning he made me get up and have sex with him and when he was done I had to cook breakfast for him.

I thought about throwing hot grits on him that day.

The only thing that stopped me was the fact that I couldn't get my kids out of the house.

He also started being nice again after that day.

After being there for a couple of hours he returned.

I told my sister what I was feeling and what I thought was about to happen.

We came up with a plan, if he came and he was acting crazy I was to stay there with her.

When he knocked on the door I could feel the energy in his knock.

As I opened up the door he tried to pull the screen door open but the screen door was locked.

I looked at him and I knew instantly something was wrong.

He said to me come on, it's time to go home.

I told him that I didn't want to go and that I was staying there.

In a split second, he turned from Doctor Jekyll to Mr. Hyde.

I Stepped back away from the door for a few seconds and I looked at him. He said to me are you serious?" I answered yes.

He started cussing me out and belittling me.

As I began to shut the door on his face he started crying.

One of his greatest performances seemed to be crying on cue.

He went from telling me how much he loved me to how much he hated me.

And how he was going to hurt me when he got his hands on me.

So I shut the door and I didn't leave with him.

A couple of hours passed and my sister and I decided to walk up to the house to make sure he didn't tear up all of my things.

I knew he was going to take what he bought for me.

I learned that over time when he gave me something and things didn't go his way he would take it back.

Lady J.

As we're walking up the street about a block away from the house I could see him going from the car to the house taking things.

As I walked up on the porch he was coming out and he had the butcher block of knives that he put in the car.

My sister and I went into the house I'm looking around.
We didn't say anything to him.

Not one word.

He's getting his things out of the house, he's walking back and forth and then he just started saying shit.

Now my sister is not a person that you could just talk shit to and not expect for her to have a rebuttal for your ass.

The next thing I know they're exchanging words back and forth and I was just standing there with my back against the wall by the door waiting for him to leave.

After he got most of his belongings and put them in his car he walked back through the house. All of a sudden he said something to my sister and then he just pushed my sister over the table. Keep in mind she's 8 months pregnant.

Then he walks over to me.
I only heard him call me and Bitch and then things got silent.

His mouth was moving but I couldn't hear his voice.
The Look on his face and the look in his eyes was pure evil, and we were standing face to face.

I said to him, Don't hit me!.

And then he…

Printed in the United States
by Baker & Taylor Publisher Services